Praises for
Let Your Lips Speak Life

Often, women experience a deficit of self-love. Sometimes, we have to say it before we hear it; hear it before we believe it; and believe it before we live it. Let Your Lips Speak Life is transformative, in that it inspires women of all ages and backgrounds to do just that!
    Dr. Shekina Farr Moore, CEO| B2F Girls

Once again, Ardre eloquently finds a way to uplift women to become their best selves. Let Your Lips Speak Life is a reminder to every woman, that love is an inside job.
    Rebecca Lynn Pope, CEO| Godly Girls

♥   ♥   ♥

Let Your Lips Speak Life is a powerful gift, that we all need each day to change our own lives, as well as the lives of others.
Yvonne Fry| Florida Commissioner on the Status of Women

Let Your Lips Speak Life is a POWERFUL book that's filled with reminders that I AM ENOUGH!
MONTSHO-ESHE| Recording Artist/Dancer

This book is an impactful tool on the journey of self-love. It is imperative that we as women, and in particular our next generation have the encouraging voice of Mrs. Orie in our arsenal. We must have messages like "Let Your Lips Speak Life" to win this war.
Sherilyn Bennett
CEO| Spiritual Sweets™ LLC

Let Your Lips Speak Life is filled with relatable wisdom for all women. This book is a powerful reminder that we must fight to love ourselves more.
Jae Nash Creator of Girl Power Hour Radio

♥ ♥ ♥ ♥

Let Your Lips Speak Life

30 DAYS OF SELF-AFFIRMING LOVE

ARDRE|ORIE

Printed in the United States of America

First Printing, 2017

ISBN: 978-0-9985210-5-3

Copyright © 2017 **Ardre Orie**

All rights reserved. No part of this publication may be reproduced, distributed, or transmitted in any form or by any means, including photocopying, recording, or other electronic or mechanical methods, without the prior written permission of the publisher, except in the case of brief quotations embodied in critical reviews and certain other noncommercial uses permitted by copyright law. For permission requests, write to the publisher, addressed "Attention: Permissions Coordinator," at the address below.

13th & Joan

500 N. Michigan Avenue, Suite #500

Chicago, IL 60611

www.13thandjoan.com

♥ ♥ ♥ ♥

This book is dedicated to the women and girls of the world. May we forever bask in our worth.

♥ ♥ ♥ ♥

Let Your Lips Speak Life

30 Days of Self-Affirming Love

Written by Ardre Orie

TABLE OF CONTENTS

Preface 11
Introduction 13
The Challenge 19
The Work 83
The Story 87
The Conclusion 99
The Impact 105
#LetYourLipsSpeakLife Challenge 107
Dear Queen 123
Endnotes 124
About the Author 125
Connect with Ardre 128

Sound the Alarm.

A **State of Emergency** has been declared on self-love.

We have before us an unraveling army. Chaos has ensued.

We are growing weary and defeat is on the horizon. War is inevitable.

There is agony and injustice. We must halt from rest. We must engulf ourselves in battle. We must hasten towards consciousness. We must remain vigilant and awake.

If we sit idle, the consequences will be disastrous.

We are indeed feeble. We have been fooled, tricked and blindsided. The pitch of the noise is deafening. The messages are evident. We have been lured into belief of false doctrines that root our existence in superficiality. It is not.

We have been coerced and convinced that our worth is synonymous with air. All lies.

Take heed and acknowledge that true riches have been reserved only for those who are awake. Those who rest will not hear, nor will their hands touch eternity.

We must acknowledge the treasures created and customized for each of us. We own the weapons to conquer; they are our birthright if only we become conscious. Intelligence, courage, grace, mercy, affection, strength and love are among our most prized weaponry. Love being the greatest of all. We must allow wisdom to guide our hands towards these weapons. We must recognize that our destiny lies in our abilities to use them. They must not remain idle. We must recognize our power. We must win the war. We must silence the noise and listen only to the heartbeat within. We must recognize and honor our value. We must discover self-love.

Introduction

The average woman sees 400 to 600 advertisements per day.(1)

It is said that before a young lady reaches the age of 17, she will have seen over 250,000 media messages and beauty ads.(2)

That means she has also been given over 250,000 ideas about what she should look like and how she should define her beauty. More importantly, she has been inundated with messages about how she should define her worth. This is dangerous. To some, media is a harmless tool, strictly reserved for entertainment and thoughtless moments to pass time. Those who are conscientious and awake, recognize that unfiltered media can make an impactful determination of one's self-worth, and ultimately, the decision making patterns that will result in either life and prosperity, or death and lack of ability to flourish. The way in which we value ourselves is just that important.

It is my belief that we deserve to create our own truths and never forget our importance. This can only be done when we are equipped with the proper tools to filter the messages that we are fed on a continual basis. At some point, we have to take a stand against the messages that we consume from mainstream media, especially if they do not mirror what we truly believe, or enhance our quality of life. Moreover, we must assume responsibility for knowing our worth. No one can do this for us.

We deserve to embark upon the infinite journey of self-discovery. We deserve to become ourselves, and accept and appreciate the set of characteristics given unto us that composes the beauty that lies within. If we do not master the ability to create filters, simultaneously remembering our worth, the alternative is imprisonment to false or imaginary societal standards.

In a world where the essence of the human existence is in direct competition with social media and technology, we are forced to determine the value of our lives. It would appear that our worth is rooted in our ability to generate an audience. Terms such as "likes" and "followers" have become synonymous with self-worth.

One might venture to say that the change makers, dream defenders and agents of peace are not relevant simply for their plight to add value to the lives of others. Mainstream media pumps our veins with the superficialities of the showcase; the veins of those who are asleep that is.

Those who are awake and conscious recognize that the keepers of destiny are those enlightened enough to master the art of self-love, free from the parameters set by the messages sent and received. If filtered and absorbed, self-love is without question, the most powerful message that we can take heed to. The power of self-love does not require validation from any other source. Those fortunate enough to hear its resounding message and beacon its call for action, journey towards a direction that no form of media can deconstruct: truth.

The greatest of all emotions is love. When given unconditionally to self, it multiplies, empowers and sustains, creating a haven of prosperity to divide and give to the world. Those who master the love of self, are those who will inevitably change the world, because the focus remains on the energy from which to create, give, share and cultivate. Those who master the love of self are filled with an infinite storage of internal resources from which to help others.

This book was created to exercise your mental ability to create filters and remember self-love. There is no greater tool to win the war.

I AM

I Always Matter

The Challenge

I challenge you to commit to 30 consecutive days of powerful mental exercises to fill your heart, mind and spirit with love, and to enhance your internal filters that protect you from the harmful effects of outside noise that is often detrimental to perception of self.

30 Days of

Self-Affirming Love

"A positive life can only be led with a positive mind."

Ardre Orie

Day 1

"My presence begins to speak before my words utter a sound."

Ardre Orie

I AM POWERFUL.

There are no external forces guiding my life that I do not allow. I am responsible for choosing the energy that is reproduced and manifested in my life. I claim superiority over negative thoughts. I trust myself and my ability to decide what is best for me. I will what I want to happen in my life. The world is my dominion and I flourish in it.

I AM Powerful.

Day 2

"The most important moment in our lives is when we realize that we deserve better."

Ardre Orie

I AM WORTHY.

I will celebrate myself. I will not await recognition or acknowledgement from others. I will bask in who and what I am. I will silence the inner critic. My only competition is in the mirror. I am the light. I approve of myself.

I AM Worthy.

Day 3

"There is no force greater than that of a woman on a mission."

Ardre Orie

I AM DETERMINED.

I will harness my full potential today. I claim victory over everything that I touch.

I will toil with dignity. I will take responsibility for my actions.

I will walk with my head held high, remembering the infinite power that grows inside of me. I live each moment with expectation of success.

I AM Determined.

Day 4

"My mind is filled with vibrant colors. I shall leave a rainbow for the world."

Ardre Orie

I AM CREATIVE.

My mind is brilliant. I will paint peace and harmony in my life like a rainbow. I will choose to activate positive thoughts. Peace and harmony will accompany me at every destination. I will breathe life into the creative genius that lives in me. My gifts and talents are infinite. I recognize that there are no problems, only opportunities.

I AM Creative.

Day 5

"I've learned to remember and recover simultaneously."

Ardre Orie

I AM HEALED.

I will relinquish my pain.

I AM not bound

I will release every hurt acquired to the skies. I will accept love. I will accept myself just as I am. I will accept the things that I cannot change. Compassion washes away pain and past hurt. I will repair myself with love.

I AM Healed.

Day 6

"I dare not take for granted the ability to feel the wind beneath my wings."

Ardre Orie

I AM ALIVE.

I will be thankful for the gift of breath. I recognize air as a divine gift. I will be present in each moment of my life. I will be an efficient steward of my time and acknowledge it as my greatest resource. I will conspire with the universe for my well being and blessings. I will illuminate a path for myself and others.

I AM Alive.

Day 7

Within, lies a treasure more precious than rubies or gold."

Ardre Orie

I AM PROSPEROUS.

I have an abundance of resources available to me. I will use my resources to fuel my dreams and invest in others. I will recognize that my prosperity is rooted in acts of kindness. I will help sow and toil with others, free from selfish gain or recognition. I will honor investments in others as an investment in myself.

I AM Prosperous.

Day 8

"When my soul speaks, I am wise enough to hear her voice."

Ardre Orie

I AM INSIGHTFUL.

I will use my words and my thoughts to will the manifestation of the desires of my heart.

I will envision my life without spiritual, emotional, physical and financial boundaries. I will chart a clear direction for my path. I will be strategic and intentional in all that I do. I will know my why.

I AM Insightful.

Day 9

I own nothing and am a steward of every-thing."

Ardre Orie

I AM WEALTHY.

I will denounce constraints and limitations on my financial, physical, mental and spiritual freedom. There is no limit to my inheritance of the world's resources. I will seek wise council to set and achieve wealth goals. I am an attractor of wealth, it flows freely into my possession.

I AM Wealthy.

Day 10

"My truest exercise of freedom is in my mind."

Ardre Orie

I AM LOGICAL.

I will use my mind as an instrument. I will be eager to expand my body of knowledge. I choose emotions wisely to accompany my thoughts. I will think before I speak, act and influence. I will be inquisitive and search for enlightenment and understanding. I will increase my levels of organization and solve my problems effectively. Everything that I need is within me. My greatest weapon is my ability to think.

I AM Logical.

Day 11

"I need only like myself."

Ardre Orie

I AM TRANSPARENT.

I will embrace myself fully. I will smile with conviction, recognizing my uniqueness. I will refrain from engagement through comparison. I will no longer hide behind false reality. I will no longer apologize for remaining true to my beliefs. I will discover who I am and I will become more of it.

I AM Transparent

Day 12

"Blessed is she who opens her soul to the universe."

Ardre Orie

I AM OPEN.

I will broaden my horizons. I will engage in behaviors to enlighten myself today. I acknowledge that wisdom rests in new knowledge. I will freely give up things that weigh me down or no longer serve me. I will become a student of the world.

I will not fear vulnerability. I will grow without boundaries.

I AM Open.

Day 13

"My secret is simple. I am humble and I am king."

Ardre Orie

I AM KIND.

Love is my birthright. I exercise compassion continually. I will speak kindly of myself and others. I vow to engage in random acts of kindness daily, recognizing that no action is too small. I will release anger and speak words of prosperity from my heart.

I will seek and reproduce nourishment from the goodness of the earth.

I AM Kind.

Day 14

"I don't have a need to accept every invitation presented. I have learned over the years, that every party does not guarantee a good time."

Ardre Orie

I AM DISCERNING.

I will filter harmful energy. I will use emotional intelligence in my daily walk. I will maneuver relationships with empathy and sound judgement. I will intentionally surround myself with people who love and encourage me. I will yield to the wisdom of my inner voice.

I AM Discerning.

Day 15

"Mercy is a hell of a gift."

Ardre Orie

I AM FORGIVING.

I will take ownership of my happiness. I will locate my points of pain and recognize them as a part of my journey. I will take an active role in my healing. I will end toxic relationships. I will envision myself mentally aligned, healthy and fulfilled. My courage outweighs my fear.

I AM Forgiving.

Day 16

"I like my water either hot or cold. Lukewarm, just won't do."

Ardre Orie

I AM COMMITTED.

If I conceive it in my heart, I will commit to achieving it with my mind. There is no obstacle that can keep me from my destiny. I will stay the course. I will not be deterred or denied. I will do what is right, not what is easy. I will choose the path less traveled. I will renew my mind, body and spirit to recharge and remain connected.

I AM Committed.

Day 17

"I can't think of one person who is worth the destruction of my peace, not one."

Ardre Orie

I AM HARMONIOUS.

I will direct my attention towards the sun. I will channel the flow of water in my soul. I hasten towards balance and inner peace. I synch with others. I exude peace. I am slow to anger and slow to speak. I emit and recycle positive energy.

I AM Harmonious.

Day 18

"She couldn't reach the top of the mountain with all of the answers in her backpack, they would weigh her down."

Ardre Orie

I AM TEACHABLE.

I will seek the guidance of my elders, recognizing the infinite wisdom that time has given unto them. I will sit at their feet and soak up their power like the sun. I will seek wisdom. I will be open to new information and the elevation of my mind. I will activate the full force of new knowledge and thrive in abundance in the presence of it.

I AM Teachable.

Day 19

"Strength is my birthright."

Ardre Orie

I AM STRONG.

I am becoming the absolute best version of myself. I will recognize and reject elements that deplete my sources of energy, happiness, joy and peace. I will imprison and suffocate self-doubt.

I AM Strong.

Day 20

"I am the anchor of my soul."

Ardre Orie

I AM GROUNDED.

I will train my eyes to recognize the blessing in every situation. I will be anchored in my spiritual and emotional beliefs. I will not sway with the wind. I am physically, mentally and emotionally connected. I will take repeated action to attract the abundance of the universe.

I AM Grounded.

Day 21

"As I stood in the crowded room, I heard someone yell out "fearless" and I turned around in haste; my name had been called."

Ardre Orie

I AM A WARRIOR.

I will harness the power within. I will arm myself with knowledge and fight my victories with power. I will stand for what is just. I will not remain silent in the presence of injustice. I will take action to maintain equality in my life and the lives of others. I will use my time, talent and resources to change the world around me.

I AM a Warrior.

Day 22

"I serve vision for breakfast, hope for lunch and victory for dinner."

Ardre Orie

I AM A LEADER.

I will own my thoughts. I will own my feelings. I will follow my instincts. I will be decisive.

I will light my path and illuminate a path for others. I will submit to the will of the universe, recognizing that I am most powerful when in sync and centered. I will be a soldier in the army for peace, positivity and righteousness.

I AM a Leader.

Day 23

I've become obsessed with being comfortable in my own skin."

Ardre Orie

I AM AUTHENTIC.

I believe in my evolution. My inner light can not be dimmed or denied. My energy is strong and pure. My intentions are good. I will walk in my truth boldly and unapologetically. I will accept myself. I am everything that I need. My DNA can not be duplicated. With it, I have the power to change the world.

I Am Authentic.

Day 24

"You won't find me sitting around, waiting for an invitation to the party. I'll simply throw my own."

Ardre Orie

I AM AMBITIOUS.

I will embody determination. I will deny mediocrity at all costs. Goal setting I will remain vigilant until a task is completed. I will be a steward of my time, talents and treasures. I will recognize roadblocks as redirection. Failure is not an option. My empire awaits.

I AM Ambitious.

Day 25

"The moment that I discovered that I had the power to make myself happy, I became free. I am no longer bound, broken, and wrapped in chains."

Ardre Orie

I AM FREE.

I will loosen the chains that bind me. I will freely release any anchor that has held me down. I will rise to the top of the ocean and walk on water. I will swim gracefully in the sea. I will give myself permission to say no. I will welcome peace, mercy and joy to surround me. I will maintain that my happiness is a direct result of the energy that I reproduce within.

I AM Free.

Day 26

"And even when the enemy attempted to destroy me, every attempt was marked, return to sender."

Ardre Orie

I AM VICTORIOUS.

I envision myself at the climax of my intentions. I am vibrating on a level far above the clouds. I align my emotions and harness my power consistently. I am elevated.

I AM Victorious.

Day 27

"I have mastered the art of suffocating fear and breathing magnificent life into faith."

Ardre Orie

I AM HOPEFUL.

I will give birth to my heart's deepest desires. I will plant seeds of greatness and water them with my work. I will anchor my mind and vibration in infinite possibilities for my life. I will not waste time in the midst of worry, I denounce it. I will visualize the evolution of what will manifest in my life. I believe in my work to make it so.

I AM Hopeful.

Day 28

"My smile set the room filled with people ablaze. They didn't know my secret. I had discovered love in the mirror".

Ardre Orie

I AM LOVE.

I will allow love to radiate through my skin. I will allow love to radiate through my soul. I will touch others with my sweet scent and leave a lasting impression. I will be patient with myself and others. I will take good care.

I AM Love.

Day 29

"I refuse to question my worth."

Ardre Orie

I AM ENOUGH.

I am not inferior to anyone or anything. Every element and manifestation in my life is a result of my thoughts and actions. I will utilize all that I have to create the best life possible for myself and others. It is ok for me to have everything that I want. My possibilities are endless. I am deserving of all that is for me.

I AM enough.

Day 30

"And if I don't love myself, in no way, shape or form could I demand so much from anyone else."

Ardre Orie

I AM.

I always matter.

The Work

"Write a thing and make it plain."

Ardre Orie

Speaking life into your destiny also means being intentional about the energy and power that you reproduce. Use the space below to create one sentence affirmations to speak into your life.

I Forgive...

_____
_____
_____
_____
_____

I Embrace

_____
_____
_____
_____
_____

I Love

_____
_____
_____
_____
_____

I Release

_____
_____
_____
_____
_____

I Accept

_____
_____
_____
_____
_____

I Praise

_____
_____
_____
_____
_____

I Proclaim

_____
_____
_____
_____
_____

The Story

I recently stumbled upon a photo of myself hugging my two daughters and my smile took up the entire distance of my face. I was a proud wife and mother. At the time, I had just resigned from my job as an Assistant Principal. This was a job that I had attended several years of college and earned 3 degrees to attain. It was a dream come true. I knew that I wanted to reach higher in my career, but I was happy to have checked it off my list. I was a climber; I was into titles and the status associated with them. I loved the work and my ability to positively impact the lives of young children and their families. I believed them to be our most valuable resource.

As I reflected deeper while holding the picture, my mind drifted to the period of life just before the photo was taken. During this time, I was pregnant with my second daughter. The pregnancy was tumultuous and I was encapsulated by a career that no longer fulfilled me. I had lost my love for a role that I held so dearly in my heart. I never saw it coming and I don't believe that I even saw the loss of love as possible. There were some changes in leadership and the working relationships for many became stifling. I was on the front lines. In the midst of the pregnancy and countless health scares, my family was noticeably more important than any prior ambition that had driven my actions previously. In a single decision, I had let it all go. I resigned from the job that I had worked so hard to attain. There was an uncanny sense of freedom in doing so, but the truth is that so much of my worth and what I believed about myself had been rooted in my career and the goals that I had chased. No one told me that resigning from my job would also mean coming face to face with my truth. No one told me that

I would be forced to simply listen to the sounds of my soul. No one told me that I would find myself searching for the meaning and purpose of my life.

As a full time wife and mother, I gave my family all that I could. I had always done so, but now there were no distractions. I was no longer climbing for status, or titles, or the achievement of professional goals. I transferred the energy into my family, relentlessly might I add. In doing so, I began to feel that I was losing my voice. I no longer knew who I was. And while many will never speak on the anxiety and bordering depression that can result from the loss of identity, I will.

I had such a sense of fulfillment from being a wife and a mother. I was destined to be those things. I was domestic, and enjoyed being the first face they saw in the mornings, and the first to pick them up from school. I loved serving my husband's food, and watching the smile on his face after preparing his favorite dishes. To serve them brought me great joy. I later realized that the goal chaser in me was not dead. Her will to make a difference in the world was ever present. I tried to suffocate her. What kind of person would not be happy just caring for their family?

As a stay at home mom, I found myself with time to just think. Prior to that , I could not recall a time that that opportunity had ever been present in my life. I had always been climbing. Countless days at the house turned into the sound of the dryer rotating, synced with the rustle of the leaves blowing across the front yard and the whistle of the wind. The silence was beautiful and disturbing. One day, the silence was so loud that I recall walking past the bathroom mirror and I caught a glimpse of someone walking by. I had not seen her before. There I was standing face to face with myself. I must have stood in front of the mirror for at least 30 minutes. I don't believe that I had ever really seen myself. I had been too busy. Tears began to stream down my face because I realized that I had never been transparent. Instead, I spent years painting rainbows over the lenses of my rose colored glasses. I was standing there, blessed beyond measure to be a full time wife, and full time mother and yet, I was still desperately in need of the mental stimulation that I had come to value in my professional role. Why? Why was so much of my value rooted in my ability to think, act and create?

Standing there, facing myself in the mirror, forced me to acknowledge the debris that I had been sweeping under the rug for so many years. My failed attempt to build a relationship with my father, who had been absent all of my life, and my struggle to forgive. The haunting memories of my mother, bludgeoned, victimized and entangled in a domestic violence filled relationship, and the fact that I had not learned to love and embrace myself, were glaring reflections that could not be denied. Those things, collectively, were the ugly truth that stared back at me in the mirror. If I were brutally honest, I really didn't recognize my reflection. For years, I had thrown myself into work and goals and "having it all", so much so, that I never took the time to just discover me. I'm not even sure if I cared to. I wiped my tears, shrugged my shoulders and enforced one of my usual "get it together girl" motions and moved on. I left her standing there in the mirror. She had to die. I wished death upon her. There was no time for this type of meltdown. Life was in motion.

The more I lost my voice, the more silent I became about the real issues and discovering who I was. I wasn't willing to do the work, to dig within to discover me. Maybe I wouldn't like what I would find. I would continue in this same self-destructive pattern, cooking harder, smiling more and working diligently to embody the "Stepford Wife Life" as I called it. My first breakthrough came unexpectedly when I decided to pen my first book. I figured that was a way to satisfy the almost dead woman within, who wanted to speak, but had been kidnapped and silenced without disrupting the flow of life for my beautiful family, who was thriving and learning and growing. I had mapped out a plan to tell the stories of 21 women and teen girls, digging deep to love the reflection that they saw in the mirror. In retrospect, it is still amazing that I selected this topic to write about because subliminally, it was my greatest struggle, but I wasn't willing to admit it. This book was about others and what they were experiencing. As I began to interview the women, I felt right at home, knowing that I was making a difference. The woman within me was actually breathing again. As I neared completion of the book, I recall sending my manuscript for review, by my then editor. Repeatedly, he would inquire about why I was passionate about writing this book in particular? He kept digging to get me to express my thoughts and sentiments on the topic and how it personally impacted me. I maintained that self-esteem and self-worth were concerns for all women, so I needed to tell these women's stories. I really didn't have the thought-provoking answer that I felt like he was digging for. My response was simply "I want to make a difference". I knew that I was impactful, because the ladies who participated in the interviews were overjoyed and expressed the burden that they felt had been lifted, when provided with the opportunity to simply tell their stories. I had arranged an entire weekend of events that would eventually develop into an annual retreat that provided the ladies with makeovers and a photoshoot, but only after we had spent time doing the work and digging into their stories the night before. The retreat stressed the importance of inner and outer beauty. During the retreat, a teen participant asked me what my story was. I couldn't muster up the first word before the tears began to stream down my face. These weren't my tears, they belonged to the woman inside of me. There was a pause filled with silence and in an instant, all eyes were on me. Before I knew it, she took her first breath and spoke her first words. Her words emerged from my mouth, "My father was not a part of my life and his absence made me feel like I was not good enough." There it was. My ugly truth. After she spoke, I took a deep breath. The air was fresh and I felt revitalized. There I sat, with tears streaming down my face and tears streaming down the faces of the other ladies, in the midst of my ugly truth. I was beautiful. She was beautiful. It was in that moment that I made the connection between myself and the woman in the mirror that I had not recognized years ago. She was me. The lightbulb also went off as to why my editor was insistent on me expressing my why for writing. The book that I was writing to "helping others", was also healing for me. God had placed me there, in that moment, to not only help others, but to experience the same freedom myself. Telling their stories was just as much about me, as it was them.

In the presence of the ugly truth, I discovered so many beautiful findings. I determined that I had worked so hard for titles and success because I never wanted to feel like I wasn't good enough. That was what my father's absence made me feel. I had learned from my mother that if you build your own castle, you never have to worry about being invited to anyone else's. Work and making a difference was what I had seen my grandmother and my mother do. They used their hands and their hearts to make their communities a special place, while giving every drop of themselves to their families. I now knew that it was ok for me to give myself permission to do the same. There was nothing wrong with wanting to stimulate my mind, body and soul, while striving for excellence and to build legacy with my family. These revelations would lead me to allow the woman inside to speak. I rediscovered my voice.

A year later, I completed my first book, Consciously Beautiful: I Am Enough. The title and every page in the book had a special meaning to me, because it was my journey towards doing the work to love the reflection in the mirror. I wanted to be proud of who I was and most importantly, I wanted to know who I was. The book release was a massive success, in part because so many women needed this same message so desperately. We just need to know that we are ok and that our feelings, that are often unexplained, are valid.

    I continued writing and found refuge in doing so. I would eventually redefine my entire career and make a living as a writer. Today, I am a full time wife and mother. These are the greatest accomplishments of my life. My family is the best reflection of what, I believe, my time here on earth was purposed for. I've also revitalized the woman living inside of me. She speaks freely. I launched a publishing company affectionately named 13th & Joan. My grandmother was born on October 13th and my mother's name is JoAnn and we often refer to her as Joan. I am the bold intersection of these two women. My journey towards loving myself was a long, winding road, and so worth it. Today, I love myself, flaws and all. I am not perfect and work daily to elevate my mind and the energy that flows from within, but the difference is how I speak to and about myself. I now recognize that our words are more powerful than ever. I speak affirmations over my life daily. This is why I felt so strongly about writing this book. If we can simply practice speaking power into our lives, a shift occurs, that can change the trajectory of our futures. Speaking positively to and about ourselves is an absolute game changer. We all have a story and we all have ugly truths, but the act of self-love is undeniably beautiful. To love ourselves is revolutionary.

The Conclusion

"There is no one like you, nor shall there ever be."
Ardre Orie

It is our responsibility to know that we are worthy. No other person in our lives can give us the satisfaction that accompanies knowing our value. When we question our worth, we do not make the best judgements in the most critical areas of our lives. In the presence of depleted self-worth, we choose wrong. I repeat, in the presence of depleted self-worth, we choose wrong. This mindset does not allow us to operate on a wavelength that vibrates high enough to overcome obstacles, avoid pitfalls and flourish. Speaking life into your existence must be a daily practice. We must remain vigilant in the exercise of filters from which to receive our messages from the world about who we are.

1. Speak life into your existence daily.

Creating healthy habits can not be optional. Before we ever set foot into the world, we are inundated with messaging that can either harm or help our disposition and beliefs about what will manifest. I have learned from experience that to have a day filled with wins, I must begin the day with winning behaviors. Affirmations is at the top of my list and sets the tone for the energy that I emit and reproduce.

2. Speak life into the existence of others.

The greatest way to rise is to lift others. There is untapped power in speaking positivity into the lives of others. For every compliment and word of encouragement that you give, there is an enormous storage of energy that awaits you. Why miss out on the opportunity to be the reason that someone smiles? It is priceless. Furthermore, when you spread positive energy, the universe conspires and the person in which you passed the energy to, now has a reserve from which to spread the wealth. Imagine if we all just threw kindness around like confetti. The world would be more colorful.

3. Fill your cup.

A friend once told me that it was not possible for me to pour from an empty cup.. Just as we are charged to pass the positivity to others, we are also responsible for executing this same act for ourselves. Taking time to gain a deeper understanding of who we are, our motivations, strengths and weaknesses, will also yield key information that can be used to determine ways to refuel and revitalize. Years ago, I began working out very early in the morning and came to treasure those moments because they allowed me time to invest in my personal health and time with my thoughts. I also learned over the years that I truly enjoy time to write my thoughts. Neither of these things cost any money but prove to be priceless in filling my cup. Take time to learn what filling your cup consists of and do more of it.

4. Sit in silence to hear the noise.

Are you able to put your phone aside and just be? We have become so engaged with our electronic devices that sitting in silence seems to be a thing of the past. Silence, however, is still a strategy of those who are most successful. Whether you decide to engage in full meditation or just simply sit in silence, doing so is impactful. There is so much substance in moments of silence.

5. Serve others.

Too often we search for purpose. I most certainly did. I failed to realize that ultimately, we have but one purpose: service. We are only gifted the experience of waking each morning because it has been ordained that we have work to do. That work is rooted in service. In these acts of kindness, we are most powerful. Close your eyes and reminisce about a time when you were in the midst of helping someone. Consider how in that moment, your problems disappeared and your heart felt the warmth of giving to others. This is the human connection with purpose. We are here to serve. Period.

6. Own your story.

If you are reading this, then you have survived what has happened to you. That alone is worthy of celebration. Life is filled with highs and lows that can often present significant challenges, but we have been given the tools that we need to weather the storm. A very significant step that can not be missed when tapping into our power is owning our stories. Far too often, we are ashamed of what has happened to us. What remains certain is that there is not one face that walks the earth that does not bear a story. We have been conditioned to just keep going through life, without acknowledging what has happened to us. I often tell my writing clients that they need to get so comfortable with their joys and pains that they can call them by name. There is power and abundance in doing so.

7. Tell your story.

True ownership of your story means that you recognize the value in telling it, because you realize that it will positively impact the life of another. Any great victory, or great valley, will prove to be inspirational to another life. We have an obligation to share in the wealth of the knowledge that we have acquired along the way. We sometimes fail to realize that we have established a blueprint for someone else in the midst of simply living our lives. Your presence in the world should make it a better place. There is someone who is traveling a similar journey that won't need to make the same mistakes. There is someone who is traveling a similar journey that will need someone to share in a joy of life that only someone who has experienced can understand. It is imperative that we share our stories. They serve as stepping stones to success and evolution.

The Impact

"The story born from the depths of a soul, is such a revelation".
Ardre Orie

It is my hope that you will recognize the value in your journey. No one has experienced life through your lens. No one. This alone makes you unique. It is my belief that when we acknowledge the value in our stories and experiences and find them worthy of sharing with the world, we all win. If you dare, I challenge you to take the #LetYourLipsSpeakLife Challenge.

For the next 7 days, I encourage you to tell your story. I have mapped out some elements that spark the evolution of

I want every woman to feel what I felt the moment I decided to speak my truths. If you dare, dive in.

#LetYourLipsSpeakLife
CHALLENGE

"The untold stories of our souls are magical blueprints for prosperity."

Ardre Orie

Day 1:

Sum up your life in one paragraph.

_____
_____
_____
_____
_____
_____
_____
_____
_____
_____
_____
_____
_____
_____
_____
_____
_____
_____
_____
_____

Day 2:

Write about your earliest childhood memory.

_____
_____
_____
_____
_____
_____
_____
_____
_____
_____
_____
_____
_____
_____
_____
_____
_____
_____
_____
_____

Day 3:

Write about you biggest disappointment.

Day 4:

Write about your greatest loss.

_____
_____
_____
_____
_____
_____
_____
_____
_____
_____
_____
_____
_____
_____
_____
_____
_____
_____
_____
_____

Day 5:

Write about your greatest win.

Day 6:

Write about what you have been most criticized for.

_____
_____
_____
_____
_____
_____
_____
_____
_____
_____
_____
_____
_____
_____
_____
_____
_____
_____

Day 7:

Write about the most influential person in your life.

Day 8:

Write about what scares you.

Day 9:

Write about what you are most grateful for.

Day 10:

Write about your enemies.

Day 11:

Write about what you chase.

Day 12:

Write about how you believe the world sees you.

_____
_____
_____
_____
_____
_____
_____
_____
_____
_____
_____
_____
_____
_____
_____
_____
_____

Day 13:

Write about how you see yourself.

Day 14:

Write about who you would be, if failure were not an option.

"To walk a thousand miles, you must be bold enough to take a single step."

Ardre Orie

Dear Queen,

If you are reading this and you have successfully taken the #LetYourLipsSpeakLife Challenge, congratulations are in order! You've written some very significant components that tell your story. I know for certain that if you wrote from your heart, you felt something. We all do when we embark upon a journey such as this. If you've come this far, I'd strongly suggest that you continue walking. Should you decide to do so and you don't want to walk alone, I will walk with you. Not only does the world need to hear your story but you deserve to #letyourlipsspeaklife

All my love,

Ardre|Orie
Writer|Publisher|Advocate

Endnotes

(1) Dittrich, L. "About-Face facts on the MEDIA." About-Face web site. [Online: http://about-face.org/r/facts/media.shtml. Last retrieved April 14, 2000]

(2) Media Influence on Teens. Facts compiled by Allison LaVoie. The Green Ladies Web Site. [online: http://kidsnrg.simplenet.com/grit.dev/london/g2_jan12/green_ladies/media/ . Last accessed April 13, 2000]

About the Author

**Celebrity Memoirist,
Playwright and Screenwriter**

ARDRE ORIE is a memoirist, playwright and screenwriter who specializes in identifying the heart of every story she tells so that they are grounded in their roots *and* amplified in their message. Her love of writing began when she wrote and published her first book at the age of ten to chronicle the narratives of accomplished black women in her community. The product of a single-parent home and childhood survivor of domestic violence, Ardre recognized that there was great power in the transparency of her pain through storytelling.

She has written for a host of clients from the WNBA, NBA, NFL, MTV, WETV, BRAVO, BET, CENTRIC, OWN, VH1, and YouTube; for Grammy Award-winning artists, political activists, and politicians; as well as a bevy of entrepreneurs and everyday heroes. Her goal as a writer is to allow the voices of those who have suffered from oppressive circumstances to be heard and to create meaningful content that feeds our souls and chronicles their experiences. Prior to taking a leap of faith toward entrepreneurship, Ardre attended Florida State University, where she earned both her undergraduate and Master's Degrees in Education. After teaching for 4 years, she went on to earn an Ed.S in Educational Leadership. Ardre Orie currently resides in Atlanta, Georgia, with her husband, two daughters, and a loving son in college.

Follow **Ardre Orie**'s *journey at*
WWW.IAMARDREORIE.COM.

CONNECT WITH ARDRE ORIE ON SOCIAL MEDIA

Website:
www.IAMardreorie.com

Facebook:
www.facebook.com/IAMardreorie

Instagram:
www.Instagram.com/IAMardreorie

Twitter:
@IAMardreorie

SERVICES

- Just Publishing
- Author Coaching
- Ghostwriting
- Author Branding
- Brand Photoshoot

- Author Coaching
- Social Media Campaigns
- DIY Publicity & Marketing

For all your publishing & author marketing needs!

WWW.13THANDJOAN.COM

Let Your Lips Speak Life

30 DAYS OF SELF-AFFIRMING LOVE

ARDRE|ORIE

www.ingramcontent.com/pod-product-compliance
Lightning Source LLC
Chambersburg PA
CBHW070626300426
44113CB00010B/1675